Natural Soap Making:

a Simple and Pure Approach for Beginners

5 EXTRA BONUS!

INSIDE THE BOOK

Make soaps without lye

Make all-natural cosmetics

Safety Charts

Oil Properties

Labels for your soaps

SCROLL TO THE END AND SCAN THE QR CODE

© Copyright 2023 by Donna Alba All rights reserved.

This document is geared towards providing exact and reliable information in regards to the topic and issue covered. The publication is sold with the idea that the publisher is not required to render accounting, officially permitted, or otherwise, qualified services. If advice is necessary, legal or professional, a practiced individual in the profession should be ordered.

- From a Declaration of Principles, which was accepted and approved equally by a Committee of the American Bar Association and a Committee of Publishers and Associations.

In no way is it legal to reproduce, duplicate, or transmit any part of this document in either electronic means or in printed format. Recording of this publication is strictly prohibited, and any storage of this document is not allowed unless with written permission from the publisher. All rights reserved.

The information provided herein is stated to be truthful and consistent, in that any liability, in terms of inattention or otherwise, by any usage or abuse of any policies, processes, or directions contained within is the solitary and utter responsibility of the recipient reader. Under no circumstances will any legal responsibility or blame be held against the publisher for any reparation, damages, or monetary loss due to the information herein, either directly or indirectly.

Respective authors own all copyrights not held by the publisher.

The information herein is offered for informational purposes solely and is universal as so. The presentation of the information is without contract or any type of guarantee assurance.

The trademarks that are used are without any consent, and the publication of the trademark is without permission or backing by the trademark owner. All trademarks and brands within this book are for clarifying purposes only and are owned by the owners themselves, not affiliated with this document.

In the hands of the maker, art takes wing,
From nature's touch, pure fragrances sing,
With care and love, gifts come alive,
In each soap, connections deeply thrive.

Lavender's grace, orange's warm tune,
Scents waltz in glow, under the moon,
Chamomile soothes, cinnamon's bold play,
Every bar tells a tale, in a unique way.

Alchemy stirs, in bubbles and blends,
Passion's mark, where the heart sends,
Eucalyptus cool, and the rose's embrace,
Each soap holds a soul, a familiar face.

In water's caress, with thoughts pure and true,
Soaps whisper tales, ancient and new,
Nature's soft kiss, embrace from a friend
In handmade soap, love cannot ever end.

TABLE OF CONTENTS

Introduction: The Art of Soap-Making: Beauty and Benefits 8

Chapter 1 9

1.1 What is Soap-making? 9

1.2 The History of Soap: A Journey Through Time Ancient Times 9

Chapter 2 11

2.1 The Ingredients - A World of Beauty and Creativity 11

2.2 Ingredient List 11

2.3 Choosing Ingredients 11

2.4 Natural Additives such as Herbs and Flowers 13

2.5 Fragrances and Dyes 14

2.6 Preparing the Ingredients 15

Chapter 3 16

3.1 Tools and Safety- Foundations for a Successful Craftsman 16

3.2 Required Tools 17

3.3 Safety Guidelines 17

Chapter 4 18

4.1 Basic Techniques - The Art of Soapmaking 18

4.2 Cold Process 19

4.3 Hot Process 19

4.4 Melt and Pour 20

Chapter 5 21

5.1 Creating Your Unique Soaps: 40 soap recipes 21

Chapter 6 41

20 Special Gift Ideas 41

Chapter 7 52

7.1 Sustainability in Soap Making: A Responsible Approach................................52

7.2 Soap Making: A Sustainable Venture 53

7.3 Stories that inspire 55

7.4 Useful Resources and Links: 59

Chapter 8 60

Soap Making Checklist 600

Chapter 9 62

9.1 Questions and Answers 622

Chapter 10 65

Natural dyes 65

Complete Glossary of Useful Terms 71

Useful Resources and Websites 73

Conclusion...73

Dear Reader,

For over a decade, I have been delving deep into the enchanting world of homemade soap making. I began this journey with the wide-eyed curiosity of a child and the burning desire to craft something with my own hands, something that was not only beautiful but also natural and practical.

In the early days, I faced many challenges, mixed wrong ingredients, and on more than one occasion produced a result that bore no resemblance to what I had envisioned. However, as time went on, what started as a mere hobby morphed into a true art form. I became intimately familiar with oils, herbs, dyes, and essences as if they were old friends, and every new bar of soap became an expression of my creativity and love for nature.

Now, with this book, I am thrilled to share everything I've learned with you. Whether you've never laid eyes on a soap mold or the thought of blending oils seems daunting, I will guide you step by step through every stage of the process. Together, we will revel in the joy of crafting unique and tailored soaps, delve into the intriguing history of this ancient craft, and who knows, perhaps you might discover a passion you never knew you had.

Get ready to dive into a world that smells of lavender, rose, mint, and so much more. Are you ready to start? Open the book and join me on this wonderful journey!

Warmly,

Donna Alba

Introduction: The Art of Soap-Making: Beauty and Benefits

Soap-making is an ancient and fascinating art, a magical process in which the simplest of ingredients are transformed into something both useful and beautiful. Imagine combining fragrant oils, aromatic herbs, and vibrant colors, blending them with love and care to craft something that not only cleanses but nourishes the skin and delights the senses. Making soap is more than merely a utilitarian skill; it's a creative journey that gives you the chance to express yourself and connect with long-standing customs. The satisfaction of watching a soap bar take shape in your hands is unparalleled, offering a profound sense of achievement.

Benefits of Homemade Soaps Homemade soaps boast numerous advantages beyond mere cleansing:

Naturalness: You can opt for pure and natural ingredients, avoiding harsh chemicals.

Customization: Every soap can be a unique masterpiece, reflecting your preferences and needs.

Eco-Friendly: Reduced environmental impact due to the use of biodegradable materials and the absence of unnecessary packaging.

Gentle to the Skin: They nourish and hydrate the skin, without drying it out, thanks to natural oils and additives.

Cost-Efficient: Once the basic ingredients are procured, crafting your soap can be a cost-effective way to always have top-quality products on hand.

Who Can Benefit from This Hobby Homemade soap making suits almost every personality, regardless of age or experience:

- **Creative People**: If you cherish handcrafting, you'll find joy in designing unique patterns, shapes, and fragrances.
- **Nature Enthusiasts**: If you favor natural and sustainable products, this is the perfect way to ensure what you use on your skin is pure and benign.
- **Gift Givers**: Creating customized soaps is a lovely way to give a thoughtful and unique gift.

Prepare to dive into one of the most rewarding and sensory adventures you can embark on.

Chapter 1

1.1 What is Soap-making?

Soap-making, or saponification, is the chemical process that occurs when a triglyceride (a fat or oil) is combined with a strong base, like lye (caustic soda, or sodium hydroxide), and water. This reaction yields glycerin and fatty acid salts, which we commonly refer to as "soap."

1.2 The History of Soap: A Journey Through Time Ancient Times

The Earliest Records

The use of soap is documented as far back as 4,000 years. One of the first civilizations, the Sumerians, used a soap-like material manufactured from animal fats and wood ash. It is also known that the ancient Egyptians used a similar substance to clean both themselves and their textiles.

The Greco-Roman World: From Hygiene to Medicine

Greeks and Romans didn't use soap for personal hygiene but primarily employed it for cleaning textiles. Galen of Pergamon, a renowned Roman physician from the 2nd century AD, wrote about soap's cleansing properties and its application in medical and therapeutic treatments.

The Middle Ages: Fluctuations and Revival

During the Middle Ages, soap usage saw its highs and lows. In certain regions of Europe, soap making thrived, while in other areas it fell out of favor due to cultural and religious shifts. However, by the 7th century, master soap-makers in Italy, Spain, and France began refining production techniques, ushering in a revival of the soap making craft.

The Renaissance: Science and Art

Soap making developed into an art and a science throughout the Renaissance. As soap-makers experimented with new materials and techniques, soap evolved into a luxury good valued for its aesthetic and aromatic qualities.

18th and 19th Centuries: Industrialization and Democratization

New production techniques were established throughout the industrial revolution in the 18th and 19th centuries, making soap more widely available. The introduction of lye enhanced the quality and reduced the costs, and soap became an essential part of daily life.

The 20th Century and Beyond: Back to the Roots

The 20th century saw soap making become highly commercialized, but there was also an increasing interest in traditional and natural methods. Traditional methods and natural ingredients were rediscovered by the modern artisanal and handmade soap movement, fusing innovation with tradition.

As you can see, the history of soap is a captivating journey across cultures, periods, and discoveries. Soap-making connects us to the past and bridges us to the future—an ancient tradition that continues to thrive in the hands of modern artisans.

Chapter 2

2.1 The Ingredients - A World of Beauty and Creativity

I'm about to embark on one of the most exciting phases of any new creation: choosing the ingredients. Each time I open the containers of my oils, herbs, fragrances, and dyes, I feel like an artist staring at an infinite color palette. I'm excited to share this world of possibilities with you right now.

Remember, each component can influence the appearance, feel, fragrance, and beneficial properties of your soap.

2.2 Ingredient List

1. **Oils and Fats:** Choose oils and fats based on the properties you want in your soap and the needs of the skin.

- **Olive Oil:** Provides softness and moisturization. Ideal for dry skin.
- **Coconut Oil:** Creates rich lather and adds hardness to the soap.
- **Shea Butter:** Nourishes the skin, making it smooth and supple.

2. **Liquids:**
- **Water:** The most common choice, used to dissolve the caustic soda.
- **Milk:** Can replace water for a creamier soap.
- **Tea/Infusions:** Offer natural scent and color.

3. **Additives:**
- **Herbs and Extracts:** For color and fragrance, such as lavender or chamomile.
- **Exfoliants:** Like oats or ground coffee for light exfoliating action.
- **Vitamins and Extracts:** Such as vitamin E or aloe extracts for added benefits.

Additives can be used to further personalize the soap, but care must be taken not to overdo it.

4. **Fragrances:**
- **Essential Oils:** For a natural scent, like lavender or peppermint oil.
- **Synthetic Fragrances:** Available in a broad range of scents, but less natural.

The choice between essential oils and synthetic fragrances depends on personal preferences and the needs of the soap.

5. **Dyes:**
- **Natural:** Such as turmeric for yellow or spirulina for green.
- **Synthetic:** Offer a wide range of vivid, vibrant colors.

You can choose between natural or synthetic dyes, depending on the look you wish to achieve.

6. **Caustic Soda:**
- Essential for the saponification process.
- The amount must be measured precisely to ensure a safe and effective soap.

2.3 Choosing Ingredients

Selecting ingredients requires careful thought about what you want to achieve with your soap. You can experiment and personalize, but it's crucial to understand the properties of each ingredient and how they interact with each other.

Types of Oils and Fats: Here are the details you need to know:

- **Olive Oil:** Used for 40-60% of the recipe, it provides moisturization. Rich in antioxidants and vitamin E.
- **Coconut Oil:** Added for 20-30%, it produces a nice lather and aids in cleaning the skin. Excellent for adding hardness to the soap.
- **Cocoa Butter:** Used at 5-15%, it makes the soap rich and creamy.

2.4 Natural Additives such as Herbs and Flowers

Natural additives can be incorporated in the following amounts:

• **Lavender:** 1 teaspoon of dried flowers per pound of oils, or 2-3 drops of essential oil per pound.

• **Chamomile**: 1-2 teaspoons of dried or powdered flowers per pound of oils.

• Rosemary: When used as an essential oil, 2-3 drops per pound of oils, or as a dried herb, 1 teaspoon per pound.

• **Calendula**: 1 teaspoon of crumbled dried flowers per pound of oils. Adds color and has soothing properties.

• **Peppermint**: 2-3 drops of essential oil or 1 teaspoon of crumbled dried leaves per pound of oils. Provides a cooling sensation.

• **Lemon:** Grated zest of 1 lemon or 2-3 drops of essential oil per pound of oils. Gives a lively and refreshing scent.

• **Sage**: 1 teaspoon of crumbled dried leaves or 2 drops of essential oil per pound of oils. Known for its antibacterial properties.

• **Poppy Seed**: 1 teaspoon of poppy seeds per pound of oils. Provides a gentle exfoliation to the soap.

• **Aloe Vera**: 2 teaspoons of aloe vera gel per pound of oils. Known for its moisturizing and soothing properties.

• **Hibiscus Flowers**: 1 teaspoon of ground dried flowers per pound of oils. Adds a pink hue and has emollient properties.

- **Eucalyptus**: 2-3 drops of essential oil or 1 teaspoon of dried leaves per pound of oils. Known for its cooling and decongestant properties.
- **Ginger**: 1 teaspoon of powdered ginger or 2-3 drops of essential oil per pound of oils. Adds a warm and spicy scent.

These additives can be combined or used singly, depending on the desired fragrance, color, and properties in the finished soap.

2.5 Fragrances and Dyes

Here's how to choose and utilize fragrances and dyes:

- **Essential Oils**: Essential oils are often used in soap making to add natural fragrances and sometimes therapeutic benefits. Here's a list of common essential oils you might consider.

They should be used at 1-3% of the weight of the oils, depending on the intensity you prefer. However, if you have a particularly sensitive skin, follow the specific guidelines for each essential oil.

Lavender: Relaxing and soothing, great for dry skin.
Lemon: Revitalizing and purifying, it adds a fresh, clean scent.
Peppermint: Cooling and invigorating, suitable for energizing soaps.
Sweet Orange: Energizing and toning, with a sweet and fruity aroma.
Tea Tree: Antibacterial and anti-inflammatory, ideal for purifying soaps.
Rosemary: Invigorating and strengthening, with a herbaceous scent.
Eucalyptus: Open and refreshing, suitable for cold or congestion relief soaps.
Ylang Ylang: Fragrant and luxurious, often used in indulgent bath soaps.
Geranium: Floral and balancing, suitable for sensitive or mature skin.
Patchouli: Earthy and sensual, used for deep and mysterious scents.
Bergamot: Citrusy and sophisticated, with a hint of sweetness.
Chamomile: Calming and soothing, ideal for sensitive or inflamed skin.
Sandalwood: Warm and enveloping, with a rich woody aroma.
Cedarwood: Masculine and earthy, often used in men's soaps.
Juniper: Fresh and slightly peppery, invigorating and refreshing.
Sage: Purifying and clarifying, with a herbaceous scent.
Vanilla: Sweet and comforting, often blended with other oils for added warmth.

Frankincense: Luxurious and meditative, with a deep and resinous scent.

Cinnamon: Spicy and warm, great for autumn or winter soaps.

Neroli: Floral and delicate, with a romantic and feminine aroma.

These essential oils can be used on their own or combined to create intricate and personalized scents.

Natural Dyes: Use it at your discretion, but typically a teaspoon of powder color per pound of oils. Turmeric for yellow, cocoa for brown, spirulina for green. More on this in a separate chapter later.

2.6 Preparing the Ingredients

Weigh Them Accurately: Use a digital scale to weigh ingredients in grams or ounces.

Heat the Oils and Fats: Warm the oils and fats in a saucepan on low heat until they are fully melted.

Prepare the Additives: If you're using dried herbs, chop them finely. If you're using powdered dyes, dilute them in a bit of water.

Accuracy is crucial in soap making. Each ingredient has a specific role, and the amounts must be measured precisely.

Chapter 3

3.1 Tools and Safety- Foundations for a Successful Craftsman

Becoming an adept soapmaker requires not only passion and creativity but also diligence and care. With the right tools and a commitment to safety standards, you will lay the foundation for creating with confidence and success. Soapmaking is an art that combines science and creativity, and with these fundamentals, you're ready to venture into this fascinating world with proficiency. Below you'll find a comprehensive guide on the essential tools and safety measures to follow.

3.2 Required Tools

The art of soapmaking demands specific tools, many of which you might already own in your kitchen. Here's the list:

1. **Digital Scale:** For accurately weighing ingredients.
2. **Kitchen Thermometer**: To measure the temperatures of oils and lye.
3. **Saucepan and Wooden Spoon:** For melting oils and stirring. Use sturdy materials like stainless steel or borosilicate glass.
4. **Electric Whisks or Immersion Blender:** To mix the lye with the oils.
5. **Soap Molds:** These can be made of silicone, wood, or plastic.
6. **Safety Goggles and Gloves:** Essential when handling caustic soda.

3.3 Safety Guidelines

Safety should always come first, especially when handling chemicals like caustic soda. Here are some key guidelines:

- **Handle Caustic Soda with Care**: It's a corrosive substance and must be treated with the utmost caution. Always wear gloves and goggles, and work in a well-ventilated area.

- **Always Add Soda to Water:** Never do the other way around, as it might cause a violent reaction.

- **Do not Use Aluminum Utensils:** Caustic soda can react with aluminum. Opt for stainless steel, glass, or durable plastic.

- **Keep Out of Reach of Children and Pets:** Make sure that children and household pets cannot access your workspace.

- **Understand first aid:** Rinse well with cold water after coming into touch with skin, and seek medical assistance if required.

Chapter 4

4.1 Basic Techniques - The Art of Soapmaking

The Art of Soapmaking Now that we've covered ingredients, tools, and safety measures, it's time to dive into the foundational techniques of soapmaking. Each technique has its unique appeal and intricacies, and I'm thrilled to share these insights with you. Before exploring each process, there's an important concept, "trace", you should be familiar with.

In soapmaking, "trace" refers to a specific stage in the mixing process. Trace occurs when the mix of oils and lye (caustic soda) has been blended to the point of turning slightly opaque and thick. When a droplet of the mix is drizzled onto its surface, it will leave a visible trace that fades slowly. It can have the consistency of whipped cream or thin mayonnaise. Reaching trace is a pivotal moment in soap creation, signaling that the blend is ready for the addition of additives like fragrances, dyes, or herbs, and can be poured into molds to harden. Trace can be "light" or "heavy" based on its consistency, and different recipes might call for different trace levels before moving to the next step.

4.2 Cold Process

This method is popular for its simplicity and swiftness.

1. **Preparation**: Weigh out 10.58 oz of olive oil, 7.05 oz of coconut oil, 3.53 oz of caustic soda, and 8.11 oz of water.
2. **Forming the Lye**: Slowly pour the caustic soda into the water, stirring until fully dissolved.
3. **Melting the Oils**: Heat the oils to 110-120°F.
4. **Combining:** Mix the lye solution with the oils, blending until trace (cream-like consistency).
5. **Additives:** Add 0.35 oz of essential oil, desired colorants, and pour into molds.
6. **Curing:** Let it harden for 24-48 hours, then unmold it and let it cure for 4-6 weeks.

4.3 Hot Process

This method is more time-consuming but immensely rewarding.

Step 1: Prepare the ingredients. In a bowl, blend the fat with any optional components. Heat to the temperature specified in the recipe. Monitor using a thermometer (ensure it doesn't touch the base).

Step 2: Gear up for safety! Wear protective goggles and gloves. Should caustic soda splash onto you, rinse immediately.

Step 3: Prepare the caustic soda. In a heat-resistant container, slowly mix the caustic soda into cold water. Wait until it reaches the desired temperature. Be wary of the fumes.

Step 4: Combine the solutions. Once at the right temperatures, slowly pour the caustic soda solution into the fat.

Step 5: Stir. Mix until the consistency mentioned in the recipe is achieved, ensuring uniform ingredient blending.

Step 6: Introduce the fragrance. If mixing time exceeds 5 minutes, add the fragrance towards the end. If under 5 minutes, add immediately after combining the solutions.

Step 7: Transfer to molds. Pour the soap into molds, leveling it out and removing any excess. If desired, shape leftover soap into small pieces or balls.

Step 8: Remove from molds. After the soap hardens (about 24 hours), carefully unmold. If challenging, consider placing molds in the freezer.

Step 9: Allow it to cure. Let the soap rest for at least three weeks. During this period, occasionally turn the soap to ensure even curing.

Step 10: Wrapping up. If you spot white powder (soda ash) on the soap, remove it by rubbing under water or with a damp cloth. Your soap is now ready for use!

4.4 Melt and Pour

This method involves using pre-made soap bases, making it ideal for beginners:

1. **Cut and Melt**: Cut 17.64 oz of the base and melt using a double boiler.
2. **Additive Incorporation**: Mix in 0.176 oz of essential oil and colorants as desired.
3. **Pour into molds**.
4. **Curing:** Allow it to cure for 4-6 hours.

Chapter 5

5.1 Creating Your Unique Soaps

Now's the time; here you will find 40 detailed recipes with all the necessary ingredients, weights, instructions, and tips to craft wonderful soaps in the comfort of your home.

- **Apricot Soap**: Nourishing and revitalizing, with apricot oil.
- **Aloe Vera Soap**: Soothing and moisturizing, perfect for sensitive skin.
- **Orange and Cinnamon Soap:** Energizing, with a warm and spicy fragrance.
- **Basil Soap:** Rich in antioxidants, with a hint of freshness.
- **Bergamot Soap:** Uplifting and fragrant, ideal for relaxation.
- **Cocoa and Mint Soap:** Indulgent and invigorating, with cocoa and mint oil.
- **Calendula Soap**: Soothing, with dried calendula flowers.
- **Chamomile Soap**: Relaxing, with a brew of genuine chamomile.
- **Cinnamon and Honey Soap:** Nourishing and aromatic, with spicy notes.
- **Carrot Soap:** Revitalizing, with fresh carrot juice.

- **Cucumber Soap:** Refreshing and moisturizing, with cucumber extract.
- **Chia Soap:** Exfoliating, with chia seeds.
- **White Chocolate Soap:** Pure indulgence, with real white chocolate.
- **Coconut Soap:** Tropically luxurious, with coconut milk.
- **Coffee Soap:** Exfoliating and revitalizing, with ground coffee.
- **Fennel Soap:** Purifying, with fennel extract.
- **Jasmine Soap**: Seductive and floral, with jasmine oil.
- **Ginseng Soap:** Energizing, with ginseng extract.
- **Lavender Soap:** Calming, with lavender essential oil.
- **Lemon and Rosemary Soap:** Invigorating, with a fresh citrus scent.
- **Licorice Soap:** Soothing and healing, with licorice extract.
- **Mallow Soap:** Softening, with mallow infusion.
- **Almond Soap**: Nourishing, with almond milk.
- **Peppermint Soap:** Refreshing and stimulating.
- **Myrrh Soap:** Luxurious, with myrrh essential oil.
- **Lily of the Valley Soap:** Sweet and spring-like, with a floral scent.
- **Papaya Soap:** Natural exfoliant, with papaya pulp.
- **Patchouli Soap:** Earthy and mysterious, with patchouli essential oil.
- **Peach Soap**: Sweet and refreshing, with peach extract.
- **Rose Soap:** Romantic, with dried rose petals.
- **Sage Soap:** Purifying, with sage infusion.
- **Sandalwood Soap:** Exotic and sensual, with sandalwood essential oil.
- **Green Tea Soap:** Antioxidant, with green tea extract.
- **Thyme Soap**: Natural antiseptic, with thyme essential oil.
- **Vanilla Soap**: Sweet and enveloping, with natural vanilla extract.
- **Red Wine** Soap: Antioxidant, with real red wine.
- **Ylang Ylang Soap**: Exotic, with the sensual fragrance of ylang ylang.
- **Ginger and Lime Soap**: Stimulating, with a touch of citrus.
- **Pumpkin Flower Soap**: Nourishing, with dried pumpkin flowers.
- **Pumpkin Soap**: Vitamin-rich, with pumpkin pulp

Note: In the realm of soap-making, precision is of utmost importance. While fractions can often be more intuitive and readily understandable at first glance, especially in settings where individuals are accustomed to traditional measurements, they don't always guarantee the required accuracy for consistent outcomes. This is why many soap-making recipes and instructions favor using percentage measurements or decimal values. These methods of measurement allow for greater accuracy, ensuring that every batch of soap retains the same properties and quality. When it comes to crafting a product that will be in direct contact with the skin, every minor variation can make a significant difference. Therefore, despite recognizing the intuitiveness of fractions, in this guide we've chosen to use percentages to ensure the highest possible quality and safety.

Recipe 1: Apricot Soap

Ingredients:

- Olive oil: 8.82 oz
- Apricot oil: 3.53 oz
- Lye (caustic soda): 3.17 oz
- Water: 7.05 oz
- Apricot essential oil: 0.353 oz

Instructions:

Follow the cold process outlined in Chapter 4.

Add apricot essential oil during the additive stage.

Pour into molds and allow it to harden for 4-6 weeks.

Tips: Apricot oil is nourishing and revitalizing for the skin.

Recipe 2: Aloe Vera Soap

Ingredients:

- Olive oil: 7.05 oz
- Coconut oil: 5.29 oz
- Aloe vera gel: 3.53 oz
- Lye (caustic soda): 2.82 oz
- Water: 6.35 oz

Instructions:

Follow the cold process outlined in Chapter 4.

Add aloe vera gel during the additive stage.

Pour into molds and allow it to harden for 4-6 weeks.

Tips: Aloe vera is soothing and moisturizing, perfect for sensitive skin.

Recipe 3: Orange and Cinnamon Soap

Ingredients:

Ingredients:

- Olive oil: 7.05 oz
- Almond oil: 5.29 oz
- Lye (caustic soda): 3.17 oz
- Water: 6.70 oz
- Orange essential oil: 0.353 oz
- Ground cinnamon: 0.176 oz

Instructions:

Follow the cold process outlined in Chapter 4.

Add the orange essential oil and ground cinnamon during the additive stage.

Pour into molds and allow it to harden for 4-6 weeks.

Tips: The combination of orange and cinnamon is energizing and has a warm, spicy scent.

Recipe 4: Basil Soap

Ingredients:

- Olive oil: 7.76 oz
- Coconut oil: 4.58 oz
- Lye (caustic soda): 3 oz
- Water: 6.70 oz
- Basil essential oil: 0.282 oz
- Dried basil leaves: 0.176 oz (optional)

Instructions:

Follow the cold process outlined in Chapter 4.

Add basil essential oil and dried leaves (if used) during the additive stage.

Pour into molds and allow it to harden for 4-6 weeks.

Tips: Basil is rich in antioxidants and adds a touch of freshness.

Recipe 5: Bergamot Soap

Ingredients:

- Olive oil: 7.41 oz
- Sweet almond oil: 4.94 oz
- Lye (caustic soda): 3.10 oz
- Water: 6.35 oz
- Bergamot essential oil: 0.423 oz

Instructions:

Follow the cold process outlined in Chapter 4.

Add bergamot essential oil during the additive stage.

Pour into molds and allow it to harden for 4-6 weeks.

Tips: Bergamot has an uplifting scent and aids in relaxation.

Recipe 6: Cocoa and Mint Soap

Ingredients:

- Olive oil: 6.70 oz
- Cocoa butter: 5.64 oz
- Lye (caustic soda): 3.17 oz
- Water: 6.70 oz
- Cocoa powder: 0.705 oz
- Mint essential oil: 0.353 oz

Instructions:

Follow the cold process outlined in Chapter 4.

Add cocoa powder and mint essential oil during the additive stage.

Pour into molds and allow it to harden for 4-6 weeks.

Tips: The combination of cocoa and mint is invigorating and indulgent.

Recipe 7: Calendula Soap

Ingredients:

- Olive oil: 7.05 oz
- Sunflower oil: 5.29 oz
- Lye (caustic soda): 3 oz
- Calendula infusion: 7.05 oz
- Dried calendula petals: 0.176 oz

Instructions:

Follow the cold process outlined in Chapter 4.

Add dried calendula petals during the additive stage.

Pour into molds and allow it to harden for 4-6 weeks.

Tips: Calendula is known for its soothing and healing properties.

Recipe 8: Chamomile Soap

Ingredients:

- Olive oil: 7.76 oz
- Hemp oil: 4.58 oz
- Lye (caustic soda): 2.96 oz
- Chamomile infusion: 6.70 oz
- Chamomile essential oil: 0.282 oz

Instructions:

Follow the cold process outlined in Chapter 4.

Add chamomile essential oil during the additive stage.

Pour into molds and allow it to harden for 4-6 weeks.

Tips: Chamomile is known for its relaxing and soothing effects on the skin.

Recipe 9: Exfoliating Coffee Soap

Ingredients:

Ingredients:

- Olive oil: 7.05 oz
- Coconut oil: 5.29 oz
- Lye (caustic soda): 3 oz
- Water: 6.35 oz
- Finely ground coffee: 1.06 oz

- Vanilla essential oil: 0.282 oz

Instructions:

Follow the cold process outlined in Chapter 4.

Add the finely ground coffee and vanilla essential oil during the additive stage.

Pour into molds and allow it to harden for 4-6 weeks.

Tips: Coffee gently exfoliates the skin, while vanilla adds a warm scent.

Recipe 10: Activated Charcoal Soap

Ingredients:

- Olive oil: 7.41 oz
- Avocado oil: 4.94 oz
- Lye (caustic soda): 3.10 oz
- Water: 6.35 oz
- Activated charcoal powder: 0.529 oz

Instructions:

Follow the cold process outlined in Chapter 4.

Add the activated charcoal powder during the additive stage.

Pour into molds and allow it to harden for 4-6 weeks.

Tips: Activated charcoal is known for its purifying and detoxifying properties.

Recipe 11: Lavender Soap

Ingredients:

- Olive oil: 7.76 oz
- Grapeseed oil: 4.58 oz
- Lye (caustic soda): 2.96 oz
- Water: 6.70 oz
- Lavender essential oil: 0.42 oz
- Dried lavender flowers: 0.18 oz (optional)

Instructions:

Follow the cold process described in Chapter 4.

Add the lavender essential oil and dried flowers (if used) during the additive stage.

Pour into molds and allow it to harden for 4-6 weeks.

Tips: Lavender has a calming scent and helps relax the mind and body.

Recipe 12: Lemon and Rosemary Soap

Ingredients:

- Olive oil: 7.05 oz
- Sunflower oil: 5.29 oz
- Lye (caustic soda): 2.99 oz
- Water: 7.05 oz
- Lemon essential oil: 0.35 oz
- Dried rosemary leaves: 0.18 oz

Instructions:

Follow the cold process described in Chapter 4.

Add the lemon essential oil and dried rosemary leaves during the additive stage.

Pour into molds and let it harden for 4-6 weeks.

Tips: Lemon is invigorating, while rosemary stimulates circulation and adds a rustic touch.

Recipe 13: Honey and Oat Soap

Ingredients:

- Olive oil: 6.70 oz
- Coconut oil: 5.64 oz
- Lye (caustic soda): 3.17 oz
- Water: 6.70 oz
- Honey: 0.70 oz
- Finely ground oat flour: 0.70 oz

Instructions:

Follow the cold process described in Chapter 4.

Add the honey and oat flour during the additive stage.

Pour into molds and let it harden for 4-6 weeks.

Tips: Oats exfoliate, and honey adds softness. Great for dry skin.

Recipe 14: Green Tea Soap

Ingredients:

- Olive oil: 7.05 oz
- Almond oil: 5.29 oz
- Lye (caustic soda): 2.99 oz
- Green tea infusion: 7.05 oz
- Dried green tea leaves: 0.18 oz

Instructions:

Follow the cold process described in Chapter 4.

Add the dried green tea leaves during the additive stage.

Pour into molds and let it harden for 4-6 weeks.

Tips: Green tea is known for its antioxidant and revitalizing properties.

Recipe 15: Rose Soap

Ingredients:

- Olive oil: 7.41 oz
- Grapeseed oil: 4.93 oz
- Lye (caustic soda): 3.10 oz
- Rose petal infusion: 6.35 oz
- Rose essential oil: 0.42 oz
- Dried rose petals: 0.18 oz (optional)

Instructions:

Follow the cold process described in Chapter 4.

Add the rose essential oil and dried petals (if used) during the additive stage.

Pour into molds and let it harden for 4-6 weeks.

Tips: The scent of roses is luxurious and refined, perfect for a special gift.

Recipe 16: Orange and Cinnamon Soap

Ingredients:

- Olive oil: 7.76 oz
- Palm oil: 4.58 oz
- Lye (caustic soda): 2.96 oz
- Water: 6.70 oz
- Orange essential oil: 0.35 oz

- Ground cinnamon: 0.18 oz

Instructions:

Follow the cold process described in Chapter 4.

Add the orange essential oil and ground cinnamon during the additive stage.

Pour into molds and let it harden for 4-6 weeks.

Tips: Orange and cinnamon create a warm and spicy scent, perfect for winter.

Recipe 17: Cucumber and Peppermint Soap

Ingredients:

- Olive oil: 6.70 oz
- Grapeseed oil: 5.64 oz
- Lye (caustic soda): 2.99 oz
- Water: 6.17 oz
- Cucumber juice: 0.88 oz
- Peppermint essential oil: 0.35 oz

Instructions:

Follow the cold process described in Chapter 4.

Add the cucumber juice and peppermint essential oil during the additive stage.

Pour into molds and let it harden for 4-6 weeks.

Tips: Cucumber hydrates, while peppermint refreshes, making it ideal for summer.

Recipe 18: Goat Milk Soap

Ingredients:

- Olive oil: 7.76 oz
- Coconut oil: 4.58 oz
- Lye (caustic soda): 2.96 oz
- Goat milk: 6.70 oz
- Honey: 0.35 oz

Instructions:

Follow the cold process described in Chapter 4, using goat milk instead of water.

Add the honey during the additive stage.

Pour into molds and let it harden for 4-6 weeks.

Tips: Goat milk is renowned for its nourishing and soothing properties.

Recipe 19: Dark Chocolate Soap

Ingredients:

- Olive oil: 7.41 oz
- Cocoa butter: 4.93 oz
- Lye (caustic soda): 3.10 oz
- Water: 6.35 oz
- Cocoa powder: 0.53 oz
- Vanilla essential oil: 0.18 oz

Instructions:

Follow the cold process described in Chapter 4.

Add the cocoa powder and vanilla essential oil during the additive stage.

Pour into molds and let it harden for 4-6 weeks.

Tips: Dark chocolate offers a rich and indulgent aroma.

Recipe 20: Mediterranean Herb Soap

Ingredients:

- Olive oil: 8.11 oz
- Sunflower oil: 4.23 oz
- Lye (caustic soda): 3.14 oz
- Water: 7.05 oz
- Mix of dried herbs (rosemary, thyme, oregano): 0.353 oz
- Lemon essential oil: 0.282 oz

Instructions:

Follow the cold process described in Chapter 4.

Add the mix of dried herbs and lemon essential oil during the additive stage.

Pour into molds and let it harden for 4-6 weeks.

Tips: This blend of Mediterranean herbs creates a fresh and invigorating scent.

Recipe 21: Lavender and Chamomile Soap

Ingredients:

- Olive oil: 7.41 oz

- Sunflower oil: 4.94 oz
- Lye (caustic soda): 3.10 oz
- Chamomile infusion: 6.35 oz
- Lavender essential oil: 0.529 oz
- Dried lavender flowers: 0.176 oz

Instructions:

Follow the cold process described in Chapter 4.

Add the lavender essential oil and dried lavender flowers during the additive phase.

Pour into molds and let it harden for 4-6 weeks.

Tips: Lavender and chamomile are known for their calming properties. Ideal before sleep.

Recipe 22: Exfoliating Coffee Soap

Ingredients:

- Olive oil: 7.05 oz
- Coconut oil: 5.29 oz
- Lye (caustic soda): 3.00 oz
- Strong brewed coffee: 6.70 oz
- Coffee grounds: 0.706 oz

Instructions:

Follow the cold process described in Chapter 4.

Add the coffee grounds during the additive phase.

Pour into molds and let it harden for 4-6 weeks.

Tips: Coffee grounds act as a natural exfoliant, perfect for removing dead skin cells.

Recipe 23: Oat Milk and Honey Soap

Ingredients:

- Olive oil: 7.76 oz
- Almond oil: 4.59 oz
- Lye (caustic soda): 2.96 oz
- Oat milk: 6.70 oz
- Honey: 0.529 oz

Instructions:

Follow the cold process described in Chapter 4, using oat milk instead of water.

Add honey during the additive phase.

Pour into molds and let it harden for 4-6 weeks.

Tips: Oat milk is gentle and soothing, ideal for sensitive skin.

Recipe 24: Beer and Cedar Soap

Ingredients:
- Olive oil: 8.11 oz
- Grape seed oil: 4.23 oz
- Lye (caustic soda): 3.14 oz
- Beer: 7.05 oz
- Cedar essential oil: 0.353 oz

Instructions:

Follow the cold process described in Chapter 4, using beer instead of water.

Add the cedar essential oil during the additive phase.

Pour into molds and let it harden for 4-6 weeks.

Tips: Beer adds lather and scent, while cedar gives a woodsy, masculine fragrance.

Recipe 25: Argan and Rose Soap

Ingredients:
- Olive oil: 7.05 oz
- Argan oil: 5.29 oz
- Lye (caustic soda): 3.07 oz
- Rose water: 6.35 oz
- Dried rose petals: 0.353 oz

Instructions:

Follow the cold process described in Chapter 4.

Add the dried rose petals during the additive phase.

Pour into molds and let it harden for 4-6 weeks.

Tips: Ideal for a touch of luxury, with moisturizing argan oil and the delicate scent of roses.

Recipe 26: Sea Salt Soap

Ingredients:

• Olive oil: 7.41 oz

• Coconut oil: 4.94 oz

• Lye (caustic soda): 3.03 oz

• Water: 6.35 oz

• Sea salt: 1.06 oz

Instructions:

Follow the cold process described in Chapter 4.

Add sea salt during the additive phase.

Pour into molds and let it harden for 4-6 weeks.

Tips: Sea salt acts as a natural exfoliant, perfect for deep cleansing.

Recipe 27: Calendula Soap

Ingredients:

• Olive oil: 7.76 oz

• Sweet almond oil: 4.23 oz

• Lye (caustic soda): 3.00 oz

• Calendula infusion: 7.05 oz

• Dried calendula petals: 0.282 oz

Instructions:

Follow the cold process described in Chapter 4.

Add the dried calendula petals during the additive phase.

Pour into molds and let it harden for 4-6 weeks.

Tips: Calendula is known for its soothing properties, ideal for sensitive skin.

Recipe 28: Aloe Vera and Green Tea Soap

Ingredients:

• Olive oil: 8.11 oz

• Sunflower oil: 4.23 oz

• Lye (caustic soda): 3.14 oz

• Green tea infusion: 7.05 oz

- Aloe vera gel: 0.706 oz

Instructions:

Follow the cold process described in Chapter 4.

Add the aloe vera gel during the additive phase.

Pour into molds and let it harden for 4-6 weeks.

Tips: Aloe vera moisturizes, while green tea provides an antioxidant effect.

Recipe 29: Lemon and Ginger Soap

Ingredients:

- Olive oil: 7.41 oz
- Coconut oil: 4.94 oz
- Lye (caustic soda): 3.10 oz
- Water: 6.35 oz
- Lemon essential oil: 0.423 oz
- Ginger powder: 0.176 oz

Instructions:

Follow the cold process described in Chapter 4.

Add the lemon essential oil and ginger powder during the additive phase.

Pour into molds and let it harden for 4-6 weeks.

Tips: The energizing scent of lemon combined with warming ginger is perfect to start the day.

Recipe 30: Peppermint Soap

Ingredients:

- Olive oil: 7.76 oz
- Grape seed oil: 4.59 oz
- Lye (caustic soda): 3.00 oz
- Water: 6.70 oz
- Peppermint essential oil: 0.353 oz

Instructions:

Follow the cold process described in Chapter 4.

Add the peppermint essential oil during the additive phase.

Pour into molds and let it harden for 4-6 weeks.

Tips: Ideal for a cooling effect, perfect on hot summer days.

Recipe 31: Honey and Spelt Soap

Ingredients:

- Olive oil: 7.05 oz
- Sweet almond oil: 5.29 oz
- Lye (caustic soda): 3.07 oz
- Water: 6.35 oz
- Honey: 0.71 oz
- Ground spelt: 0.35 oz

Instructions:

Follow the cold process outlined in Chapter 4.

Add the honey and ground spelt during the additives stage.

Pour into molds and let it harden for 4-6 weeks.

Tips: The spelt provides a gentle exfoliating effect, while honey moisturizes the skin.

Recipe 32: Activated Charcoal and Tea Tree Oil Soap

Ingredients:

- Olive oil: 8.11 oz
- Coconut oil: 4.23 oz
- Lye (caustic soda): 3.14 oz
- Water: 7.05 oz
- Activated charcoal powder: 0.35 oz
- Tea tree essential oil: 0.28 oz

Instructions:

Follow the cold process outlined in Chapter 4.

Add the activated charcoal powder and tea tree essential oil during the additives stage.

Pour into molds and let it harden for 4-6 weeks.

Tips: Activated charcoal is known for its ability to absorb impurities, while tea tree oil has antibacterial properties.

Recipe 33: Lavender and Chamomile Soap

Ingredients:

• Olive oil: 7.41 oz

• Avocado oil: 4.94 oz

• Lye (caustic soda): 3.07 oz

• Chamomile infusion: 6.70 oz

• Lavender essential oil: 0.35 oz

Instructions:

Follow the cold process outlined in Chapter 4.

Add the lavender essential oil during the additives stage.

Pour into molds and let it harden for 4-6 weeks.

Tips: The combination of lavender and chamomile provides a calming effect, perfect for a relaxing evening bath.

Recipe 34: Vanilla and Cocoa Soap

Ingredients:

• Olive oil: 7.76 oz

• Cocoa butter: 4.58 oz

• Lye (caustic soda): 3.10 oz

• Water: 6.70 oz

• Vanilla essence: 0.28 oz

• Cocoa powder: 0.35 oz

Instructions:

Follow the cold process outlined in Chapter 4.

Add the vanilla essence and cocoa powder during the additives stage.

Pour into molds and let it harden for 4-6 weeks.

Tips: A rich and enveloping aroma makes this soap a perfect gift.

Recipe 35: Olive Oil and Thyme Soap

Ingredients:

• Extra virgin olive oil: 12.35 oz

• Lye (caustic soda): 3.17 oz

- Water: 6.35 oz
- Dried thyme leaves: 0.21 oz

Instructions:

Follow the cold process outlined in Chapter 4.

Add the dried thyme leaves during the additives stage.

Pour into molds and let it harden for 4-6 weeks.

Tips: Thyme offers antibacterial properties and a refreshing, natural fragrance.

Recipe 36: Coffee and Shea Butter Soap

Ingredients:

- Olive oil: 7.76 oz
- Shea butter: 4.58 oz
- Lye (caustic soda): 3.03 oz
- Fresh coffee: 7.05 oz
- Coffee grounds: 0.35 oz

Instructions:

Follow the cold process outlined in Chapter 4.

Add the coffee grounds during the additives stage.

Pour into molds and let it harden for 4-6 weeks.

Tips: Coffee grounds act as a natural exfoliant, while shea butter moisturizes the skin.

Recipe 37: Orange and Cinnamon Soap

Ingredients:

- Olive oil: 7.41 oz
- Jojoba oil: 4.94 oz
- Lye (caustic soda): 3.10 oz
- Water: 6.35 oz
- Orange essential oil: 0.35 oz
- Cinnamon powder: 0.18 oz

Instructions:

Follow the cold process outlined in Chapter 4.

Add the orange essential oil and cinnamon during the additives stage.

Pour into molds and let it harden for 4-6 weeks.

Tips: Perfect for a warming and festive aroma.

Recipe 38: Goat Milk and Honey Soap

Ingredients:

- Olive oil: 7.76 oz
- Coconut oil: 4.58 oz
- Lye (caustic soda): 3.00 oz
- Goat milk: 6.70 oz
- Honey: 0.53 oz

Instructions:

Follow the cold process outlined in Chapter 4, replacing water with goat milk.

Add the honey during the additives stage.

Pour into molds and let it harden for 4-6 weeks.

Tips: Goat milk makes the soap incredibly creamy and nourishing.

Recipe 39: Aloe Vera and Eucalyptus Soap

Ingredients:

- Olive oil: 7.41 oz
- Sunflower oil: 4.94 oz
- Lye (caustic soda): 3.03 oz
- Aloe vera juice: 6.70 oz
- Eucalyptus essential oil: 0.28 oz

Instructions:

Follow the cold process outlined in Chapter 4, using aloe vera juice instead of water.

Add the eucalyptus essential oil during the additives stage.

Pour into molds and let it harden for 4-6 weeks.

Tips: Aloe vera has soothing properties, while eucalyptus opens the respiratory tract.

Recipe 40: Rose and Pink Clay Soap

Ingredients:

- Olive oil: 8.11 oz
- Sweet almond oil: 4.23 oz
- Lye (caustic soda): 3.14 oz
- Rose petal infusion: 7.05 oz
- Pink clay: 0.35 oz

Instructions:

Follow the cold process outlined in Chapter 4.

Add the pink clay during the additives stage.

Pour into molds and let it harden for 4-6 weeks.

Tips: This luxurious and delicate soap is perfect for a special gift or indulgent treat.

Chapter 6

20 Special Gift Ideas

Each of these recipes is carefully crafted to capture the essence of the occasion, using natural dyes combined with unique fragrances and textures.

Christmas: Peppermint soap with green dye.

Valentine's Day: Rose soap with red dye.

Anniversary: Vanilla and lavender soap with purple dye.

Birthday: Tropical fruit soap with rainbow dyes.

Maternity: Oatmeal and honey soap with ivory dye.

Father's Day: Sandalwood soap with brown dye.

Mother's Day: Jasmine soap with pale pink dye.

Easter: Lemon soap with yellow dye.

Wedding: White musk soap with pearly white dye.

Children's Day: Berry soap with vibrant dyes.

Halloween: Pumpkin soap with orange dye.

Graduation: Green tea soap with light green dye.

Baby Shower: Chamomile soap with blue or pink dye.

Grandmother's Day: Olive oil soap with olive green dye.

Grandfather's Day: Tobacco and leather soap with dark brown dye.

Thanksgiving: Cinnamon and apple soap with brick red dye.

Women's Day: Orchid soap with deep pink dye.

Lovers' Day: Chocolate and strawberry soap with dark red dye.

Spring Festival: Wildflower soap with pastel dyes.

New Year's Eve: Golden champagne soap with gold dye.

Recipe 1: Christmas Peppermint Soap

Ingredients:

- Olive oil: 7.05 oz
- Coconut oil: 3.53 oz
- Lye (caustic soda): 2.82 oz
- Water: 5.99 oz
- Peppermint essential oil: 0.53 oz
- Natural green dye (chlorophyll): 0.071 oz

Instructions:

Follow the cold process, mixing the green dye with the oils before adding the lye solution.

Add the peppermint essential oil during the additives phase.

Pour into Christmas molds and let it harden for 4-6 weeks.

Tips: Ideal as a Christmas gift, with a refreshing mint fragrance.

To give it as a present it: Place the soap in a transparent bag adorned with snowflake designs. Add a green ribbon and a small Christmas decoration like a fir tree or star. You can also include a tag with a festive message.

Recipe 2: Valentine's Day Rose Soap

Ingredients:

- Olive Oil: 7.76 oz
- Sweet Almond Oil: 4.59 oz

- Caustic Soda: 3.00 oz
- Rose Petal Infusion: 7.05 oz
- Natural Red Dye (paprika): 0.106 oz

Instructions:

Follow the cold process, blending the red dye with the oils.

Pour into heart-shaped molds and let it cure for 4-6 weeks.

Tips: Perfect for a romantic gift with a gentle rose aroma.

To give it as a present: Package the soap in a heart-shaped box, lined with dried rose petals. Wrap with a red satin ribbon and add a small heart-shaped tag with a love note.

Recipe 3: Anniversary Vanilla and Lavender Soap

Ingredients:

- Olive Oil: 7.05 oz
- Jojoba Oil: 4.23 oz
- Caustic Soda: 2.93 oz
- Water: 6.35 oz
- Vanilla Essential Oil: 0.282 oz
- Lavender Essential Oil: 0.247 oz
- Natural Purple Colorant (grape juice): 0.141 oz

Instructions:

Follow the cold process, mixing the purple dye with the oils.

Add essential oils during the additive phase.

Pour into elegant molds and let it cure for 4-6 weeks.

Tips: Ideal for celebrating a special anniversary with a sweet and calming scent.

To give it as a present: Place the soap in an elegant box, perhaps lined with purple silk paper. Add some dried lavender flowers and tie with a purple silk ribbon. You can also include a handwritten note for a personal touch.

Recipe 4: Birthday Tropical Fruit Soap

Ingredients:

- Olive Oil: 6.70 oz

- Coconut Oil: 4.94 oz
- Caustic Soda: 3.00 oz
- Tropical Fruit Juice: 6.35 oz
- Natural Dyes: Red (paprika) 0.035 oz, Yellow (turmeric) 0.035 oz, Blue (spirulina) 0.035 oz

Instructions:

Follow the cold process, dividing the soap into three parts and mixing each colorant in separately.

Pour in layers into molds to create a rainbow effect.

Let it cure for 4-6 weeks.

Tips: A cheerful and festive birthday gift with an exotic tropical fruit scent.

To give it as a present: Place the soap in a colorful bag, accompanied by a small bottle of tropical juice or a cocktail umbrella for a festive theme. Add a cheerful greeting card and wrap with a shiny ribbon.

Recipe 5: Maternity - Oat and Honey Soap with Ivory Dye

Ingredients:
- Olive Oil: 7.05 oz
- Coconut Oil: 4.23 oz
- Caustic Soda: 3.00 oz
- Water: 6.35 oz
- Ground Oats: 0.706 oz
- Honey: 0.53 oz
- Natural Ivory Dye: 0.071 oz

Instructions:

Follow the cold process, incorporating oats, honey, and dye.

Pour into heart-shaped molds and let it cure for 4-6 weeks.

To give it as a present: Package in a box decorated with baby imagery and tie with an ivory ribbon. Add a sweet note dedicated to the new mother.

Recipe 6: Father's Day - Sandalwood Soap with Brown Dye

Ingredients:

- Olive Oil: 7.41 oz
- Almond Oil: 3.88 oz
- Caustic Soda: 3.10 oz
- Water: 5.99 oz
- Sandalwood Essential Oil: 0.53 oz
- Natural Brown Dye: 0.106 oz

Instructions:

Follow the cold process, incorporating sandalwood essential oil and dye.

Pour into a mold of your choice and let it cure for 4-6 weeks.

To give it as a present: Place in an elegant box with wooden designs and tie with a brown ribbon. Add a card with a loving message for Dad.

Recipe 7: Mother's Day - Jasmine Soap with Pale Pink Dye

Ingredients:

- Olive oil: 7.76 oz
- Coconut oil: 4.59 oz
- Lye (caustic soda): 3.04 oz
- Water: 6.70 oz
- Jasmine essential oil: 0.706 oz
- Pale pink dye: 0.071 oz

Instructions:

Follow the cold process, incorporating the jasmine essential oil and dye.

Pour into floral molds and allow it to cure for 4-6 weeks.

To give it as a present: Place in a delicate box with floral designs and tie with a pink ribbon. Add a sentimental note for Mom.

Recipe 8: Easter - Lemon Soap with Yellow Dye

Ingredients:

- Olive oil: 8.11 oz
- Argan oil: 3.53 oz
- Lye (caustic soda): 3.07 oz
- Water: 6.17 oz

- Lemon essential oil: 0.53 oz
- Natural yellow dye: 0.071 oz

Instructions:

Follow the cold process, incorporating the lemon essential oil and dye.

Pour into egg-shaped molds and allow it to cure for 4-6 weeks.

To give it as a present: Package in an Easter-themed box, decorated with bunnies and eggs. Add a yellow ribbon and a festive note.

Recipe 9: Wedding - White Musk Soap with Pearly White Dye

Ingredients:
- Olive oil: 7.76 oz
- Coconut oil: 4.59 oz
- Lye (caustic soda): 3.17 oz
- Water: 6.70 oz
- White musk essential oil: 0.706 oz
- Pearly white dye: 0.106 oz

Instructions:

Follow the cold process, incorporating the white musk essential oil and dye.

Pour into elegant molds and allow it to cure for 4-6 weeks.

To give it as a present: Package in a sophisticated box with pearl details and tie with a white ribbon. Add a romantic note for the newlyweds.

Recipe 10: Children's Party - Berry Soap with Bright Dyes

Ingredients:
- Olive oil: 7.05 oz
- Sunflower oil: 4.94 oz
- Lye (caustic soda): 3.00 oz
- Water: 6.35 oz
- Berry essence: 0.53 oz
- Bright dyes (red, blue, green): 0.071 oz each

Instructions:

Follow the cold process, incorporating the essence and dyes.

Pour into animal-shaped molds and allow it to cure for 4-6 weeks.

To give it as a present: Place in clear bags and tie with colorful ribbons. Add labels with fun animals.

Recipe 11: Halloween - Pumpkin Soap with Orange Dye

Ingredients:

- Olive oil: 7.05 oz
- Coconut oil: 3.88 oz
- Lye (caustic soda): 3 oz
- Water: 6.17 oz
- Pumpkin essence: 0.53 oz
- Natural orange dye: 0.106 oz

Instructions:

Follow the cold process, incorporating the pumpkin essence and dye.

Pour into Halloween-themed molds and allow it to cure for 4-6 weeks.

To give it as a present: Wrap in black and orange paper and tie it with a Halloween-themed ribbon.

Recipe 12: Graduation - Green Tea Soap with Green Dye

Ingredients:

- Olive oil: 7.41 oz
- Sunflower oil: 4.23 oz
- Lye (caustic soda): 3.07 oz
- Water: 6 oz
- Green tea essence: 0.706 oz
- Natural green dye: 0.106 oz

Instructions:

Follow the cold process, incorporating the green tea essence and dye.

Pour into graduation cap molds and allow it to cure for 4-6 weeks.

To give it as a present: Place in a black box and tie with a golden ribbon, add a congratulations note.

Recipe 13: Baby Shower - Chamomile Soap with Pink or Blue Dye

Ingredients:

- Olive oil: 7.76 oz
- Almond oil: 3.88 oz
- Lye (caustic soda): 3.17 oz
- Water: 6.35 oz
- Chamomile essence: 0.53 oz
- Natural pink or blue dye: 0.106 oz

Instructions:

Follow the cold process, incorporating the chamomile essence and chosen dye.

Pour into baby-themed molds and allow it to cure for 4-6 weeks.

To give it as a present: Wrap in baby-themed gift paper, tie with a matching ribbon, and add a greeting card for the new parents.

Recipe 14: Grandmother's Day - Olive Oil Soap with Olive Green Coloring

Ingredients:

- Olive oil: 10.58 oz
- Caustic soda: 3.53 oz
- Water: 6.70 oz
- Natural olive green coloring: 0.106 oz

Instructions:

Follow the cold process, incorporating the olive green coloring.

Pour into heart-shaped molds and let it cure for 4-6 weeks.

To give it as a present: Wrap in olive green paper and tie with a gold ribbon, include a heartfelt note.

Recipe 15: Grandfather's Day - Tobacco and Leather Soap with Dark Brown Coloring

Ingredients:

- Olive oil: 7.41 oz
- Coconut oil: 3.88 oz
- Caustic soda: 3.17 oz
- Water: 6.35 oz
- Tobacco essence: 0.353 oz
- Leather essence: 0.353 oz
- Natural dark brown coloring: 0.106 oz

Instructions:

Follow the cold process, incorporating the tobacco and leather essences and the coloring.

Pour into rectangular molds and let it cure for 4-6 weeks.

To give it as a present: Wrap in brown paper and tie with a ribbon, add a caring note.

Recipe 16: Thanksgiving - Cinnamon and Apple Soap with Brick Red Coloring

Ingredients:

- Olive oil: 7.05 oz
- Almond oil: 4.23 oz
- Caustic soda: 3.17 oz
- Water: 6.17 oz
- Cinnamon essence: 0.353 oz
- Apple essence: 0.353 oz
- Natural brick red coloring: 0.106 oz

Instructions:

Follow the cold process, incorporating the cinnamon and apple essences and the coloring.

Pour into autumn-themed molds and let it cure for 4-6 weeks.

To give it as a present: Wrap in orange or brown paper and tie with a Thanksgiving-themed ribbon.

Recipe 17: Women's Day - Orchid Soap with Intense Pink Coloring

Ingredients:

• Olive oil: 7.05 oz

• Coconut oil: 4.23 oz

• Caustic soda: 3 oz

• Water: 6.35 oz

• Orchid essence: 0.353 oz

• Natural intense pink coloring: 0.071 oz

Instructions:

Follow the cold process, incorporating the orchid essence and coloring.

Pour into floral molds and let it cure for 4-6 weeks.

To give it as a present: Package in an elegant box with pink tissue paper and tie with a silk ribbon. Add a note dedicated to extraordinary women.

Recipe 18: Valentine's Day - Chocolate and Strawberry Soap with Dark Red Coloring

Ingredients:

• Olive oil: 6.35 oz

• Cocoa butter: 4.94 oz

• Caustic soda: 3 oz

• Water: 6.35 oz

• Chocolate essence: 0.353 oz

• Strawberry essence: 0.177 oz

• Natural dark red coloring: 0.106 oz

Instructions:

Follow the cold process, incorporating the essences and coloring.

Pour into heart-shaped molds and let it cure for 4-6 weeks.

To give it as a present: Package in a romantic box with dried rose petals. Tie with a red ribbon and include a love letter.

Recipe 19: Spring Festival - Wildflower Soap with Pastel Coloring

Ingredients:

• Olive oil: 7.05 oz

• Almond oil: 4.23 oz

• Caustic soda: 3 oz

• Water: 6.35 oz

• Floral essential oils blend: 0.53 oz

• Natural pastel coloring: 0.106 oz

Instructions:

Follow the cold process, incorporating the essential oils and coloring.

Pour into flower-shaped molds and let it cure for 4-6 weeks.

To give it as a present: Package in a canvas bag with a pastel ribbon. Add a card with a spring greeting.

Recipe 20: New Year's Celebration - Golden Champagne Soap with Gold Coloring

Ingredients:

• Olive oil: 7.05 oz

• Grape seed oil: 4.23 oz

• Caustic soda: 3 oz

• Champagne: 6.35 oz (replace water)

• Natural gold coloring: 0.106 oz

Instructions:

Follow the cold process, incorporating the champagne and coloring.

Pour into festive molds and let it cure for 4-6 weeks.

To give it as a present: Package in a gold box with shimmering stars. Tie with a gold ribbon and add a New Year's greeting card.

I hope these special soaps make these occasions truly fragrant!

Chapter 7

7.1 Sustainability in Soap Making: A Responsible Approach

As worldwide awareness of environmental and social concerns grows, we are driven to consider our choices as makers as well as consumers. Even if soap making might seem like a small piece in the vast mosaic of sustainability, every decision we make carries an impact. The ingredients we select, the sources from which we procure them, and the practices we embrace can make a difference. Our area of influence may look small as home-based makers, yet each soap we make is a statement, a manifestation of the values that we hold dear.

The Modern Era and the Role of Ethics and Sustainability

In the present age, sustainability and ethics have emerged as pivotal terms in goods production. Therefore, it's fitting to have a chapter that discusses this topic in a straightforward yet informed manner. Growing environmental awareness, along with concerns about human rights and working conditions, has encouraged both consumers and producers to reconsider old manufacturing and consumption techniques. Big corporations as well as small artisans and local enterprises are increasingly engaged in this paradigm shift.

Within the unique domain of soap making, these principles take on specific importance. Soap has an old history that may be traced back to numerous cultures and civilizations. However, with industrialization and mass manufacturing, many time-honored, sustainable traditions were abandoned in favor of faster, cheaper alternatives, often at the expense of the environment and people.

Key Concepts of Sustainability

1. **Definition of Sustainability**: Sustainability can be described as the capacity to maintain or support a process or state over time. In

environmental terms, it refers to utilizing natural resources in ways that can cater to both present and future generations.

2. **The Three Pillars of Sustainability**: The classic model of sustainability is anchored in three intertwined pillars:

Environmental: This pertains to the safeguarding of ecosystems, biodiversity, and the atmosphere. It emphasizes reducing pollution, advocating renewable energy use, and diminishing our ecological footprint.

- **Social:** This centers around the well-being of individuals and communities. It encompasses themes like equity, education access, justice, health and wellness, and human rights.
- **Economic:** This concerns the prudent management of resources and economic balance. It signifies that economic practices must be structured to be sustainable in the long run, without depleting resources or causing economic harm.

3. **The Importance of Sustainability**: Lacking sustainability, we're at risk of exhausting the very resources that sustain us. Here are reasons why it's crucial:

- **Resource Conservation for Future Generations**: It's our responsibility to ensure that coming generations have access to the resources essential for a high quality of life.
- **Biodiversity**: Every life form on Earth is interconnected. Losing one species can trigger ripple effects on other species and the entire ecosystem.
- **Climate Change**: Unsustainable resource use, especially fossil fuels, has ushered in climate changes that now threaten our security, health, and environment.
- **Social Equity and Justice**: Managing resources and the economy sustainably can help reduce inequalities and ensure access to opportunities for all.

7.2 Soap Making: A Sustainable Venture

In today's world, sustainability has become a motto for many people. This concept transcends mere recycling or using biodegradable products. It is about developing a future in which natural resources are used wisely, ensuring the well-being of both present and future generations. But how does this all relate to the world of handmade soap?

1. **Waste Reduction**: Homemade soap presents a significant opportunity for waste reduction. Consider the vast amount of plastic wrappers and containers discarded annually due to industrial soaps. By crafting your own soap, you can opt for reusable or entirely biodegradable packaging, thus lowering the ecological footprint.
2. **Ingredient Control**: Making soap at home gives you complete control over the components used. This makes sure you can avoid harsh chemicals, synthetic dyes, or fragrances that may affect not only the skin but also the environment when washed away. You can support farmers and manufacturers who use ethical practices by embracing natural, organic, and sustainable ingredients.
3. **Reducing Pollution**: Industrial soap production demands energy, often from non-renewable sources, and can release harmful chemicals into the environment. Making soap at home diminishes demand for such products, subsequently reducing associated pollution.
4. **Customization and Educational Value**: Making soap at home not only allows you to personalize items, it is also an educational experience. Experimenting with different recipes teaches you about the qualities of various ingredients and their interactions. Such craft can also be used to educate the youth about chemistry, sustainability, and the importance of making environmentally responsible decisions.

Soap making is more than just an art or a hobby – it's an opportunity. An opportunity to make a difference, to make choices that reflect who we are, and the world we wish to nurture. As we continue on this journey, let's remember that every small act matters, and our dedication to sustainability and ethics can illuminate the path for many others

7.3 Stories that inspire

While there are several stories about the quest for a greener planet, some stand out for their creativity, tenacity, and impact. The three tales that follow are brilliant examples of individuals and initiatives who have made sustainability their credo, proving that it is possible to build a sustainable and prosperous future with devotion and ingenuity. Let their journeys and visions for a better world inspire you.

Clara's Green Beginnings

Clara was born and raised in Maine, with the Atlantic Ocean crashing on the shoreline. She used to collect seashells and wonder at the immensity of the ocean as a youngster, which motivated her to become a marine scientist. Her studies on microplastics revealed the devastating impact of human activity on marine life. During a conference, Clara was particularly struck by a statistic highlighting just how much chemical runoffs from commercial soaps contributed to the deteriorating health of aquatic ecosystems.

This knowledge fueled a determination within Clara. She began researching soap making, reading old books, attending workshops, and joining online communities. The beginning was anything but easy. In her small kitchen, with pans and pots doubling as mixing containers, she faced multiple failed attempts. From uneven textures to soaps that wouldn't cure, the challenges seemed endless.

Her commitment to sustainability posed yet another hurdle. Due to its connection with deforestation and habitat destruction, the extensive use of palm oil in traditional soap production raised ethical questions. Clara was determined to find an alternative. On a field trip studying marine flora, she had an epiphany about the potential of seaweed extracts. Rich in minerals and having natural moisturizing properties, seaweed became the star ingredient of her soap line.

However, introducing a novel ingredient had its setbacks. Clara had to convince potential customers about the benefits of seaweed, in a market dominated by fragrant and colorful commercial soaps. She organized workshops, educating people about the environmental costs of their choices and the advantages of natural ingredients.

Gradually, word spread about Clara's unique seaweed-infused soaps. Her brand garnered attention from local markets to artisanal shops in big cities. Emphasizing transparency, Clara provided detailed information about her sourcing methods, ensuring customers of the ethical production process.

Clara has shown that with determination and a clear vision, it's possible to blend business with environmental sustainability, creating ripples of positive change.

Raj's Medicinal Mission

Raj grew up in the busy center of Mumbai, among the city's vivid bustle. He would frequently retreat to his grandmother's tranquil garden as a child, where he learnt about the numerous medicinal plants and their age-old uses. This early exposure combined with his academic pursuit in pharmacy led Raj to appreciate the wonders of traditional Indian herbs deeply.

His path took a personal turn when his beloved grandmother developed a severe skin allergy. Doctors prescribed numerous ointments, but nothing seemed to alleviate her discomfort. Raj, driven by love and his pharmaceutical knowledge, recalled a family recipe that incorporated specific herbs into soap. He believed that the consistent use of such a medicinal soap might provide the relief his grandmother desperately sought.

However, turning a generations-old recipe into a market-ready product was no easy task. Raj's first batches, while effective, lost much of the medicinal potency of the herbs during the saponification process. To keep the medicinal essence of the plants, he spent many hours improving the approach, working with traditional healers and contemporary scientists alike.

Another challenge was the market's inclination towards flashy commercial soaps. Raj's herbal soaps, on the other hand, had earthy tones and delicate aromas that did not instantly appeal to the public. Educating people about the long-term advantages of natural substances over quick-fix, chemically-induced remedies became an essential part of his mission.

Raj's unwavering commitment to sustainability gave him an edge. In an era when customers were growing more mindful of their environmental impact, Raj forged partnerships with local farmers. This not only ensured the organic cultivation of herbs but also supported a fair trade model, uplifting the rural farming community. As news spread about Raj's soap's healing properties, testimonials from delighted consumers began to flow in. Tales of skin ailments being alleviated and general skin health improving became synonymous with Raj's brand. Raj's environmentally friendly and ethical approach began to draw a loyal consumer base that respected both the product's benefits and its sustainable ethos.

Amelia's Artistic Adventure

Amelia's artistic soul flourished amid the steel skyscrapers and screaming traffic of New York City. Her paintings, as a great visual artist, reflected the city's liveliness in vibrant strokes. Amelia's creative instincts, however, were not limited to paints and brushes. She longed to create everyday items with an artistic flair, which led her to the ancient and transformational realm of soap making.

It began in a rather casual way, as a small weekend project. Amelia's soaps showcased whirls of colors and intricate patterns inspired by nature and urban life. She incorporated natural dyes and often found herself lost in the rhythm of creating something that was both beautiful and functional. However, making soap was not without challenges. Amelia's first soaps, while visually captivating, didn't always hold up in daily use. The balance between creating a lasting piece of functional art and maintaining its aesthetic integrity was a continuous learning curve.

The fast-paced world of commercial soap making added to her struggles. Amelia's handcrafted soaps, each a work of love and time, looked out of place in a metropolis where everything moved at breakneck pace. She was frequently under pressure from competing with commercial brands that produced generic soaps at a fraction of the time and cost.

However, the universe had a unique way of guiding Amelia. The spark for change was an unexpected opportunity to attend a seminar on sustainable soap making. Here, Amelia was introduced to the holistic philosophy of zero-waste production, which resonated deeply with her values. Determined to merge her artistry with sustainability, Amelia revamped her production process. She introduced soaps that were free of toxic chemicals, molded them in reusable silicone molds, and took extra care in wrapping them in biodegradable materials. Her unique soaps quickly became popular. Pop-up kiosks displaying her works became a common sight at New York's farmer's markets and art festivals. People were drawn not just to the aesthetic appeal of her soaps but also to the story behind each bar - a tale of art, dedication, and a commitment to the environment.. Her story emphasizes that, even in a rapidly changing urban landscape, there's room for artisanal craftsmanship, heart, and a touch of nature's magic.

Useful Resources and Links:

Ethical Consumer's Guide to Soap:
- www.ethicalconsumer.org: A guide reviewing the ethical practices of various soap brands.

Fair Trade Certified:
- www.fairtradecertified.org: Information on choosing Fair Trade certified ingredients and their positive impact on producing communities.

Rainforest Alliance:
- www.rainforest-alliance.org: A resource for sourcing sustainable ingredients that protect forests and communities.

These resources represent just the tip of the iceberg of what's available for those looking to make a difference in the soapmaking world. The key is knowledge and action; to learn and then to apply what you've learned. With dedication and commitment, every soapmaker can contribute to a more sustainable world.

Chapter 8

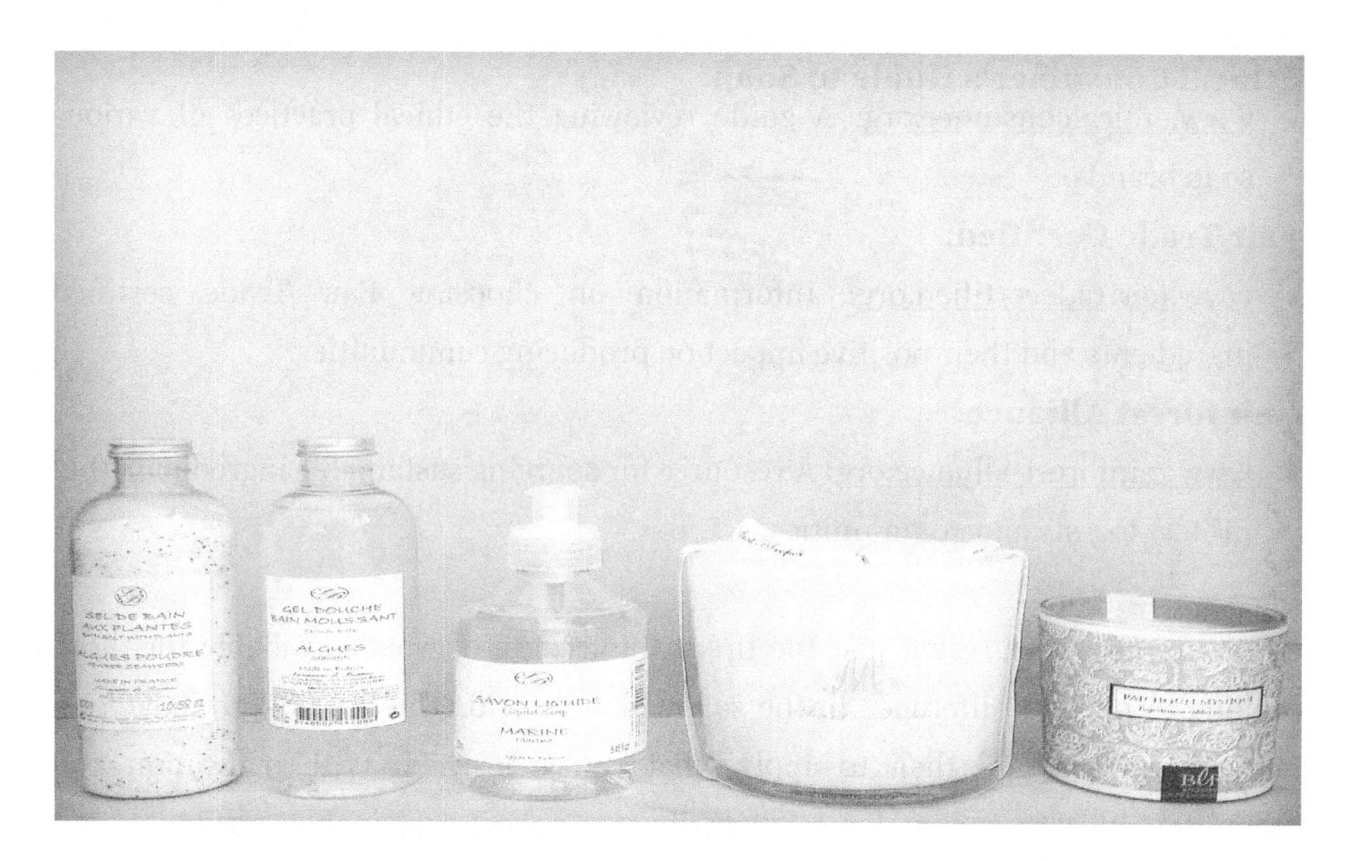

Soap Making Checklist

This checklist will be invaluable in ensuring you have everything you need and follow the correct procedure:

Preparation:

- **Recipe:** Choose a specific recipe to follow.
- **Ingredients:** Ensure you have all the oils, butters, lye (caustic soda), water, additives, and colorants required.
- **Equipment:** Set out pots, spoons, thermometers, scales, stick blender, molds, and protective glasses and gloves.
- **Workspace:** Clean and organize your working area.

Soap Creation:

- **Weigh Ingredients:** Accurately weigh oils, lye, and water.
- **Melt the Fats:** Heat the oils and butters to the specified temperature in the recipe.

- **Prepare the Lye Mixture:** Dissolve the lye in water, observing safety precautions.
- **Blend Fat and Lye:** When both reach the desired temperature, combine the lye mixture with the oils.
- **Blend to Trace:** Use a stick blender to mix until the mixture reaches trace (whipped cream consistency).
- **Add Additives:** If needed, add colorants, fragrances, herbs, or other additives.
- **Pour into Molds:** Transfer the mixture into your prepared molds.
- **Cover (if required):** Some recipes may ask you to cover the molds to retain heat.

Curing:

Cut the Soap (if necessary): After 24-48 hours, remove the soap from the molds and cut into bars.

- **Allow it to Cure:** Place soap bars in a dry, ventilated area, letting them mature for the required period (e.g., 4-6 weeks for the cold process).
- **Check:** Ensure the soap is fully cured before using or packaging.

Safety Precautions:

- **Protective Glasses and Gloves:** Always wear them when working with lye.
- **Adequate Ventilation:** Work in a well-ventilated area, especially when preparing the lye mixture.
- **Proper Labeling and Storage:** Store and label ingredients correctly.

By following this checklist, you should be able to safely and effectively craft handmade soap!

Chapter 9

This chapter is designed as a quick reference to address the most common problems you might encounter. With practice and attention to detail, you'll be able to craft beautiful and functional soaps with both success and satisfaction.

9.1 Questions and Answers

- **Can I substitute one oil for another?** Yes, but it's crucial to understand the properties of each oil. Some might be more moisturizing, while others could produce better lather. Use an online soap calculator to help with the proportions.
- **How long should I let the soap harden?** Typically 4 to 6 weeks, but it depends on the recipe and process. Always follow specific guidelines for each recipe.
- **Can I use food coloring in my soaps?** It's better to use soap-specific dyes as food colorings can react unpredictably with other ingredients.
- **Can I make soap without lye?** Lye is vital for the saponification process. However, there are premade soap bases available that you can melt and customize with scents and colors.
- **How do I know if I've used too much lye?** An excess of lye will make the soap hard and potentially irritating. Use an online soap calculator for the right proportions.
- **Do homemade soaps have an expiration date?** Homemade soaps typically last between 1 to 2 years when stored correctly. Adding antioxidants like vitamin E can extend their shelf life.
- **Can I use essential oils in my soap?** Yes, essential oils are a great choice for scenting your soap. However, use them sparingly, as they can be potent.
- **What can I use as soap molds?** You can use specific soap molds or everyday items like yogurt containers or ice trays, as long as they're heat-resistant and won't react with the soap mixture.

- **How can I make my soap more moisturizing?** Adding oils like olive oil or shea butter can make your soap more moisturizing.
- **What if my soap doesn't harden?** It might need more time, or there might be an issue with ingredient proportions. Review the recipe and ensure all instructions were followed correctly.
- **Is it normal for my soap to sweat?** Soap "sweating" is often due to glycerin attracting moisture. It can be common, especially in humid environments.
- **Can I make soap with kids or pets in the house?** Yes, but it's crucial to adhere to strict safety guidelines, especially concerning the use and storage of lye.
- **Can I use cooking oils for soap making?** Yes, many cooking oils like olive oil and coconut oil can be used, but it's essential to check the appropriate proportions for each type.
- **My soap's color changes over time. Is that normal?** Yes, some dyes might fade or change over time. Using soap-specific colorants can help maintain the color.
- **How can I test the pH of my soap?** You can use pH testing strips, available online or in specialty stores, to check your soap's alkalinity.
- **How can I prevent air bubbles in my soap?** Pouring slowly and tapping the soap mold gently can reduce air bubbles.
- **Can I make soap without using molds?** Molds help give a consistent shape, but you can hand-shape soaps or use other containers.
- **How can I further customize my soaps?** You can add ingredients like oats, herbs, or clay for additional texture and benefits.
- **How long should I wait before using my homemade soap?** The wait varies based on the method used. Cold process typically requires a 4-6 week "curing" period.
- **Can I remelt a soap that didn't turn out well?** Yes, soap can be remelted, but adjustments to ingredients might be needed.

- **Is it possible to make liquid soap instead of bar soap?** Yes, the process is different and requires specific ingredients, but it's definitely doable.
- **How can I tell if my soap is safe for sensitive skin?** Use gentle ingredients and test the soap on a small skin area before using it all over the body to ensure it's suitable for sensitive skin.

Chapter 10

Natural dyes

A chapter on natural dyes couldn't be missing. Here, you'll find the knowledge and skills required to add a colorful touch to your homemade soaps. Through detailed instructions, practical tips, and precautions, you'll safely and successfully venture into the world of natural dyes.

Dyes from Plants and Flowers:

Rose:

• Preparation: Soak rose petals in warm water for 24 hours.

• Color: Pale pink.

• Amount: 1 tablespoon of petals per 100g of soap.

• Note: You can intensify the color using darker rose petals.

Spinach:

• Preparation: Boil spinach leaves and strain the liquid.

- Color: Green.
- Amount: 2 tablespoons of liquid per 100g of soap.

Dyes from Spices and Herbs:

Turmeric:

- Preparation: Use turmeric powder.
- Color: Bright yellow.
- Amount: 1/4 teaspoon per 100g of soap.

Cocoa Powder:

- Preparation: Mix directly into the soap.
- Color: Brown.
- Amount: 1 teaspoon per 100g of soap.

Saffron:

- Preparation: Soak in hot water.
- Color: Golden yellow.
- Amount: A few strands per 100g of soap.

Paprika:

- Preparation: The paprika powder can be added directly.
- Color: Orange.
- Amount: 1/2 teaspoon per 100g of soap.

Dyes from Fruits and Berries:

Blueberries:

- Preparation: Blend blueberries and strain the juice.
- Color: Blue or purple.
- Amount: 3 tablespoons of juice per 100g of soap.

Strawberries:

- Preparation: Use strained strawberry juice.
- Color: Red.
- Amount: 3 tablespoons per 100g of soap.

Dyes from Vegetables:

Beetroot:

- Preparation: Blend beetroot and strain the juice.
- Color: Pink or red.

- Amount: 3 tablespoons per 100g of soap.

Carrots:

- Preparation: Use strained carrot juice.
- Color: Orange.
- Amount: 2 tablespoons per 100g of soap.

Dyes from Minerals and Earths:

Clay:

- Preparation: Choose differently colored clays, such as green or pink.
- Color: Varies.
- Amount: 1 teaspoon per 100g of soap.
- Note: Mix the clay with a bit of water before use.

Zinc Oxide:

- Preparation: Use in powder form, mixed with a bit of water.
- Color: White.
- Amount: 1/2 teaspoon per 100g of soap.

Sienna Earth:

- Preparation: Use in powder form.
- Color: Natural brown.
- Amount: 1 teaspoon per 100g of soap.

Dyes from Common Foods:

Black Tea:

- Preparation: Infuse 1 tea bag in 1 cup of boiling water and let it cool.
- Color: Dark brown.
- Amount: 2 tablespoons per 100g of soap.
- Preparation: Use finely ground coffee or concentrated coffee.
- Color: Deep brown.
- Amount: 1 tablespoon per 100g of soap.

Lemon Juice:

- Preparation: Squeeze directly from the fruit.
- Color: Pale yellow.
- Amount: 1 tablespoon per 100g of soap.

Special Dyes for Special Occasions:
- **Christmas:** Combine spinach green with beetroot red.
- **Valentine's Day**: Use rose petal pink with strawberry red.

Mixing Colors in Soaps:

Mixing colors in soaps is a sophisticated technique allowing for unique shades and hues, personalizing the final product.

Understand Color Theory

Before starting, it's crucial to understand the basic concepts of color theory:
- **Primary Colors**: Red, Yellow, and Blue. They cannot be achieved by mixing other colors.
- **Secondary Colors**: Created by mixing two primary colors (Green, Orange, and Purple).
- **Tertiary Colors**: Created by mixing a primary color with an adjacent secondary color.

Choosing the Right Dyes

Dyes can be synthetic or natural. For a more organic approach, you can opt for natural dyes such as:
- **Red:** Beetroot, Paprika.
- **Yellow:** Turmeric, Saffron.
- **Blue:** Spirulina, Red Cabbage (with alkaline pH).
- **Green:** Chlorophyll, Seaweed.

Mixing Techniques

- **Gradual Addition**: For shades, add the dye gradually, testing on a small sample.
- **Use of a Mortar**: For uniform colors, mix the pigments in a mortar before adding them to the soap mixture.
- **Filtering**: If using natural materials, filter the mixture to avoid lumps.

Creating Shades and Tints

- **Lighter Shades**: Add white (like titanium dioxide) or use less dye.
- **Darker Shades**: Increase the amount of dye or add a bit of black.
- **Custom Tints**: Experiment by mixing primary, secondary, and tertiary colors.

Intensity Control
- **Light**: For detailed designs and bright colors.
- **Heavy**: For deeper and defined colors.

Safety and Testing
- **Patch Test:** Always test a small amount to check the color reaction.
- **Safety:** Use gloves and goggles when handling dyes, especially synthetic ones.

Recording and Documentation
Keeping a record of proportions and techniques used can help replicate or modify colors in the future.

Preparation of Natural Dyes
Red (Paprika or Beetroot):
- Paprika: Mix 1 tablespoon of paprika powder with 2 tablespoons of olive oil, heat in a double boiler, and filter.
- Beetroot: Grate and finely chop the beetroot, cover with water and bring to a boil. Reduce and simmer until the water turns red. Filter the liquid.

Yellow (Turmeric or Saffron):
- Turmeric: Mix 1 tablespoon of turmeric powder with 2 tablespoons of hot water.
- Saffron: Soak saffron threads in hot water until the water turns yellow.

Blue (Spirulina or Red Cabbage):
- Spirulina: Mix 1 tablespoon of spirulina powder with 2 tablespoons of water.
- Red Cabbage: Finely chop the cabbage and cover with water. Cook until the water turns blue (with alkaline pH).

Green (Chlorophyll or Seaweed):
- Chlorophyll: Purchase liquid chlorophyll or extract from finely chopped green leaves soaked in alcohol, then filter.

- Seaweed: Grind the seaweed into a fine powder and mix with a small amount of water.

Mixing and Blending

Prepare the Soap Base: Follow your favorite soap recipe, using cold or hot methods, until you reach a "light trace".

Add the Dyes: Divide your soap into separate bowls for individual coloring. Add the previously prepared dyes, mixing well.

Create Shades: For lighter or darker shades, add more or less dye, or use titanium dioxide or a natural black dye.

Pouring Techniques: Use techniques like layered pouring, angle pouring, or the "swirl" to create unique designs.

Harden and Cut: Allow the soap to harden as per your recipe's instructions, then cut into desired shapes.

Packaging and Labeling: Package the soap attractively and include labels with ingredients, especially if it's intended as a gift.

Note:

The amount of dye to use will vary depending on the desired shade and the type of soap you're making. It's always a good idea to conduct small tests to determine the correct proportions for your specific project.

Practice and experimentation are key in this creative process

Complete Glossary of Useful Terms

Here is a glossary of the most common terms in soap making:

Additives: Substances like herbs, flowers, and fragrances added to soap to enhance its appearance, smell, or therapeutic properties.
Base: The blend of oils and fats that form the main structure of the soap.
Emulsifier: A substance that helps to mix ingredients that don't normally combine well, such as water and oil.
Essences: Essential oils or fragrances used to give soap a pleasant scent.
Lye: The result of mixing an alkaline base (like caustic soda) with water.
Mold: The form used to shape the soap.
Essential Oils: Concentrated oils extracted from plants used to scent soap.
pH: Measure of the acidity or alkalinity of a substance.
Hot Process: Soap making method that involves cooking the ingredients.
Cold Process: Soap making method that does not require cooking: the chemical reaction happens naturally.
Saponification: The chemical reaction that occurs when a base (oil/fat) combines with an alkaline substance, turning it into soap.
Caustic Soda: Alkaline substance (sodium hydroxide) used in making hard soaps.
Superfatting: Adding extra oil to the recipe that remains in the finished product, making the soap more moisturizing.
Trace: A phase in the soap making process in which the mixture starts to thicken, indicating that saponification is underway.
Vitamin E: Natural antioxidant often added to soaps to extend their shelf life.

Useful Resources and Websites

NOTE: The author of this book is not affiliated with any of the websites mentioned in the list.

Soap Making Forum (soapmakingforum.com): An active forum where soap makers can exchange ideas, resources, and tips.

Bramble Berry (brambleberry.com): A leading supplier of soap making ingredients, including oils, dyes, and molds.

Soap Queen (soapqueen.com): A blog run by the founder of Bramble Berry, with tutorials, recipes, and soap making advice.

The Handcrafted Soap & Cosmetic Guild (soapguild.org): An organization offering support, insurance, and training for soap makers.

Lovin' Soap Studio (lovinsoap.com): Provides online courses, free tutorials, and resources for soap making.

Nature's Garden (naturesgardencandles.com): A supplier of materials for making soaps, candles, and homemade cosmetics.

Modern Soapmaking (modernsoapmaking.com): An educational resource with courses, articles, and tools for soap makers of all levels.

Wholesale Supplies Plus (wholesalesuppliesplus.com): A wholesale supplier of ingredients for soap making, cosmetics, and bath products.

From Nature With Love (fromnaturewithlove.com): A company providing organic and natural ingredients for soap and cosmetic production.

Soap Making Resource (soap-making-resource.com): An online resource with recipes, guides, and a store for soap making enthusiasts.

Conclusion

As we reach the end of this soap making guide, it's useful to stop and consider the fascinating union of art and science that creates each soap bar as a unique and unmatched masterpiece. Throughout this book, we've embarked on an adventure of discovery, spanning from time-honored methods to natural ingredients, from advanced techniques to the captivating tales behind this ancient craft. Yet, beyond the techniques and formulas, it's the artisan's heart and passion that breathes life into every soap bar.

This book was painstakingly crafted with love and dedication, with the aim of educating and inspiring. Making soap is more than a science, it is a ritual that honors nature in all its splendor.

I sincerely hope that this book becomes a trustworthy companion at your side, as you delve further into the world of soap making. Every soap you craft will be a chapter of your unique story, a tale of dedication, curiosity and a love for natural beauty. And as you express yourself through the art of soap making, keep in mind that every creation carries a piece of your heart and soul.

Embrace every step of the process, take pride in every triumph, and view each challenge as an opportunity for growth. Share your creations with the world, and bestow joy and well-being through your hands.

Finally, I want to express my heartfelt gratitude for choosing to embark on this journey with me. Every adventure needs a companion, and I am honored that you've chosen this book as yours. Look forward with passion and wonder, and always remember that for every query or doubt, you will find guidance here. Thank you for allowing me to be a part of your soap making journey. Until our next adventure together!

SCAN THE QR CODE
TO GET BONUS CONTENT!

OR COPY AND PASTE THE URL:

https://drive.google.com/drive/folders/104eS4lL4YHZavpug53Ov0iESrhU9fsg4?usp=sharing

Made in the USA
Middletown, DE
31 October 2023

41718038R00044